POEMS WORTH SAVING

ABIGAIL DE NIVERVILLE

To my former self, who carried me through it all.

POEMS WORTH SAVING

I intend to fill this world
with all that I am
and have never been.

———

I've imagined you in different ways
in the window
on the street
in passing cars
holding me with your gaze.
I reach out my hand for you to take
you don't see
you don't see so much
and I see everything
feel everything that wounds me.

Sitting on the front steps
spring breeze on our faces
I say
"those are forget-me-nots,"
point to the tree
where Nick planted them once
"...will you forget me?"

You never speak
I know the answer.

————

A heart with stained glass walls
still beats
still bleeds
still shrieks.

In the dead of night
(in darkness)
I had my first kiss.
I thought I'd never have it.
Not then.

Not like that.

———

I am leading a double life.
One foot: the city
One foot: the coast

City
in its concrete neon
forests of colour and darkness
storms of loneliness and elation
choruses of screams
from trains and cars
and people too—
all screaming.

Coast
in its bright loneliness
the blue waves rolling
through summers and winters
grey and calm
yet shrill in my ears
pulsating in my spirit.

Each life is contained
they rarely intersect
brief cracks in the map.

How can people
exist in two worlds?

I know it's possible.

And yet
we are
in different worlds
different lives.

How I wish
he'd reach out
to the city
and make this double life
single.

———

I'll send you bits of poems:
my life
hasn't quite become
something
to write home about.

———

I fell in love with a monster
he didn't expect
what I'd eventually
become.

———

My first kiss
was stolen from me.
It can't be brought back
I can never choose
a different path.

And that won't make
all the difference.

———

How can you wish someone well
and still
want them
to burn?

———

I've erased myself
to be someone else
someone
easier to love
at least
someone easier
to *keep*.

———

He said
he'd never forget the night he
"made me a woman."

Made.

What did he make?
A wretched monster?
A creation abandoned
when he saw what he'd done?

Made.

His touch
reducing me
into corners of rooms
transparent
and fragile?

No.

I was already a woman.
He didn't take anything from me
except my time,
didn't make anything of me
except a wreckage
or a monster
or a ghost.

I'd rather
become a monster
than a ghost.

———

I think I understand
Sandy at the end of *Grease*.

If all your life
people saw you as
"innocent and sweet,"
wouldn't you rebel?
Wouldn't you seek ways
to erase that?

She took Danny
to give her edge
he wasn't enough.

She saw Rizzo
and dreamed
of the girl she could be
if only
she looked
the part…

She said goodbye
to her old self
to feel something new
to be someone new
to be taken seriously
for once
in
her
life.

I shed my old self
like Sandy at the end of *Grease*
but he still saw me
as Sandra Dee.

———

I had a dream about you
not because I missed you
not because
I was afraid
of what I realize you'd been.

I felt nothing.

That's what you are
to me.

———

This city is mine:
for all that I am and am not
it stands.

The streets are here to know
and explore
and commit
to memory.

I will never forget
how it feels
to return
after being home.

*(It's hard to say
where home is now)*

Ever since he left
I see that home
still feels
like two places.

*(I don't think that's bad
anymore)*

I thought
he was home
because I missed him
so much.

(He was a wound)

I once thought
home was a person.

(Maybe for some)

I was taught
home was a partner
and maybe
sometimes it is.
But not him.

Now,
I pray for
my family.

I pray
we will always
be happy.

———

We were friends
now we're not.
I don't know how it happened.
But I'm honestly glad
it broke so gradually.
I didn't want to burn
that bridge.

I was weary
of crossing it.

———

If he can't say "I love you"
what's
the fucking
point?

———

Understand
the love has been burned
from my heart.

That doesn't mean
I will let that stop me.

I move slowly,
cautiously,
eyes wary—
my mouth isn't as open
as it may have been once,
my heart isn't as full
as it may have been once.

I am trying
to plant the garden
once more.

———

Life is cruel
and you are not
still, I am cruel to you.

Like a wave
that crashes on a rock
I beat
and beat
you down.
But a rock is resilient
it never breaks
only
changes.

You only change
with every breath I take
I am a bomb
you let me detonate
over
and over again.

Never ceasing,
I am the seasons
but you are the weather,
ever-changing
never fading.

Tell me
what's your secret?

———

I don't want
to make him human
to open the wound
to imagine the alternative.

That maybe he was
the fallen hero—
that I
judged half the story
cold
stone-hearted
unwilling to open
my mind
to other narratives.

No.

He forgot
the light that shone within me
he forgot
the soul that shattered
by his hand.

He doesn't deserve
to be human
ever again.

———

I need to fall in love
quietly,
softly,
arms wrapped around me,
warmth settling in me.

A love that is gentle,
creeps up on me:
butterflies and smiles
and knowing
just
knowing.

I need to find
the love I've dreamed
the love I denied myself
the first time.

Maybe I will fail
again
and again.
I must strive
to find the imagined.

I need to believe
someone like that
can be real —
that love isn't meant
to be quivering hearts,
bleeding uncertainty.

That love is more
than mixed messages
deciphering codes.

I need to believe
it could happen to me.

———

There is a church in my heart.
Here will I call
"sanctuary."
Here will I lie down and pray
the sun will shine on me.

———

I've killed you
in my mind
a thousand times.

It's not imagining
a blade
cutting through
or bullets
cascading down.

No,

I've brought out the worst of you
hung it to dry
let it settle
in my bones
on my tongue.

It's how I'll remember you
maybe not how you were
but how time shaped you
into the tragedy
I've become.

———

I'm tired
of being yours.
You stopped being mine
long ago
but I'm still
yours.

I hate that.

In everything I do
there's a second
there's a moment
I wonder
what you'd say.

I don't want to be yours
since you
were never mine.

I want to be mine
and pretend
I was never
yours.

———

I want someone to hold me—
the scene playing in my head
has a blurred face
a masked voice.

I want to see
someone real for once
I can't even see you.

There is nothing
I feel nothing
I want to feel something—
if I do for too long
I know
I have to feel nothing.

Feeling nothing
is better than something
that makes you fear the burning flame
so much
you won't even light a candle.

Don't let me
sabotage myself.

———

I am the warrior princess
don't you forget it.
In a gown
and a crown of flowers
I will fight
all that devours me.

And I will keep my soft laugh
though life has aged me.
And I will keep my tenderness
in a world of pure cruelty.

I am not
as I seem.

———

The devil lives
in the town I called home.
In his own way
he comes for everyone.

The skies are grey
the marsh is deep
and none of us
can ever
sleep.

None of us
can ever
dream.

And yet
we are never
awake.

———

I faced
the giant beast:
the stone forest
of lonely souls.

Alone,
isolated,
I learned to love it.

Let it swallow me up
spit me out
change me
into someone hardened
soft
passionate
unafraid
elbows jutted out
voice raised
yelling at doors closing in my face.

Who I was before,
I haven't been
have never been
for most of my life.

Lay her to rest,
open your eyes
and find me.

See how I live
in the mouth
of the beast.

———

I'm sorry
I love my dreams
more
than I ever loved you.

———

Don't crash through
my stained glass walls
this sanctuary
this church in my heart.

You don't
have to break me
to find
what lies beneath.

Can't you see
the beauty of it all?
This encased heart
of wrought-iron
and glass?

I will show you my heart.
Don't you want it
to last?

You don't need
to break open
this glass casing.
I'm not some damsel
waiting to be freed.

I built this myself
rebuilt it again
this paradise
this refuge.
And I will open the doors
when I choose.

Be kind
patient
understand:
I'm not looking
to be swept off my feet
ever again.

———

Look like the innocent flower,
But be the serpent under it.

Sorry,
but fuck that.
I'm sick
of looking sweet
with the bite underneath.

I want them to look
and know
I could cut.

I'm done painting
the image all wrong—
won't hide anymore
the fury inside
with a smile.

I want them
to know
who's coming.

———

I was made
from mud and clay:
salt water
air
flowing in my veins.

I was made
from taxis
skylines
memories of cities
I've never seen.

There's a voice calls me
away
away
from seashells
salt
mud
clay.

Calls me onward
onward
to the city born into me.

Two worlds
bridge my soul:
two lines converge
where stoplights
meet stars
and stars
fall away.

———

If we all went
to Monet's garden—
what would we see?

Not
what he saw
never
like he saw it.

If we painted
Monet's garden
what would he see?

Flower
tree
garden path?
A hidden emotion
no one
can ever
find?

Does a flower
mean a flower
or does it mean
something different
to everyone?

You have no right
to come back to me
now I'm on the edge
of my dreams.

———

Everyone is moving ahead,
I am trapped—
not sure what
has ensnared me
this time.

But I am not
who you believe me to be
and I can't
believe in me
for a moment
to finally speak.

So I stay
breathe
take this time
wait this time
for the right time
to open everything
and let it all flow free
like the river my soul has become
I want to drench the world with my heart
I want to feel the world feel me and know me
I want to be unafraid for once
I am too unlike my stories.

———

I will make myself
beautiful
ugly
untouchable
unbreakable
fragile
whole
unimaginable.

I have warred with myself
long enough
to know
I am beautiful
and yet
I don't want that
to be
the only part
you see.

Please
(oh, please)
don't ask that
of me.

———

I will never
wither away.

———

I don't want
to write words
about my body
give it praise
power
might.

I understand
for some
that brings comfort
security
pride.

But me...
I don't want to *be* my body.
It is the host
for my mind
my spirit
it could've been put in any body
it was placed in this one
this will carry me home.

I am more than my body
I am more than even my heart
I am what I leave behind
and I intend to leave
something
worth
saving.

———

I'm waiting
for my first kiss
everything that came before
I've obliterated -
it's gone
I've thrown it away
not something to be cherished.

I'll imagine
I still have a chance
of that scene under the stars
in the back of some old pickup truck
as we uncover
secrets unknown to us.

I'll imagine
the scene has a soundtrack—
soft voice on the radio
lyrics perfectly synced—
I'm wearing my favourite
something.

Sober, content,
hesitate—
wait
til I say "yes."

I won't fear to open my heart
or my book
or my hand:
take it all
kiss it
and whisper
"you've always been
brilliant."

"I know."

———

ACKNOWLEDGMENTS

Writing is hard, and writing poetry is even harder. I'd like to acknowledge the people out there who helped me actually hit "publish" when I'd doubted myself for so long.

A huge thank-you to my fellow poet and editor Shelby Eileen, for giving me much-needed praise and criticism right when I needed it the most.

To Ceillie Simkiss, for formatting the ebook and saving me so much pain and misery.

To Cristina Nikolic, for the beautiful cover photo and design. I'm a bit awkward when it comes to posed photos, but you made me feel at home.

To my best friend Ael who read all my poems over the years (even the cringe ones) and never stopped encouraging me.

To my family, who was always there for me.

And to you, the reader, for being here too. May we all find peace.

ALSO BY ABIGAIL DE NIVERVILLE

I Knew Him (*Ninestar Press, 2019*)

ABOUT ABIGAIL DE NIVERVILLE

Abigail de Niverville is an author, composer, and poet based in Toronto, Canada. Born on the East Coast, Abigail draws inspiration from her experiences growing up there. When she's not writing words frantically, she composes music and holds an M.Mus from the University of Toronto.

Her debut novel *I Knew Him* was released in 2019 by NineStar Press and is available through most major book retailers.

* 9 7 8 1 5 2 0 7 4 6 8 8 3 *